THE OFFICIAL
CHELSEA FC
ANNUAL 2023

Written by **Richard Godden** and **Dominic Bliss**

Designed by **Daniel May**

A Grange Publication

© 2022. Published by Grange Communications Ltd., Edinburgh, under licence from
Chelsea FC Merchandising Limited. www.chelseafc.com. Printed in the EU.

ISBN 978-1-915295-41-5

Welcome to The Official Chelsea FC Annual 2023!

It's been another action-packed year for the Blues, in which we became champions of the world after lifting the FIFA Club World Cup for the first time in our history.

You can relive that incredible moment in Abu Dhabi, and get the low-down on our current men's and women's players, plus the new ownership of Chelsea Football Club. We'll check out who's coming through from the Academy and get an insight into what makes Mason Mount, Thiago Silva and Sam Kerr so special. You can also find out about some of the most memorable moments from the club's history.

It's been 25 years since we won the European Cup Winners' Cup and the UEFA Super Cup in 1998, and 40 years since Clive Walker scored the goal that saved Chelsea from dropping into the third tier of English football. Then we'll be looking back at 30 years of the Premier League – and Chelsea have been there since the start!

We've got loads of quizzes, games and top facts too. So, what are you waiting for? Let's get stuck into the latest Chelsea Annual!

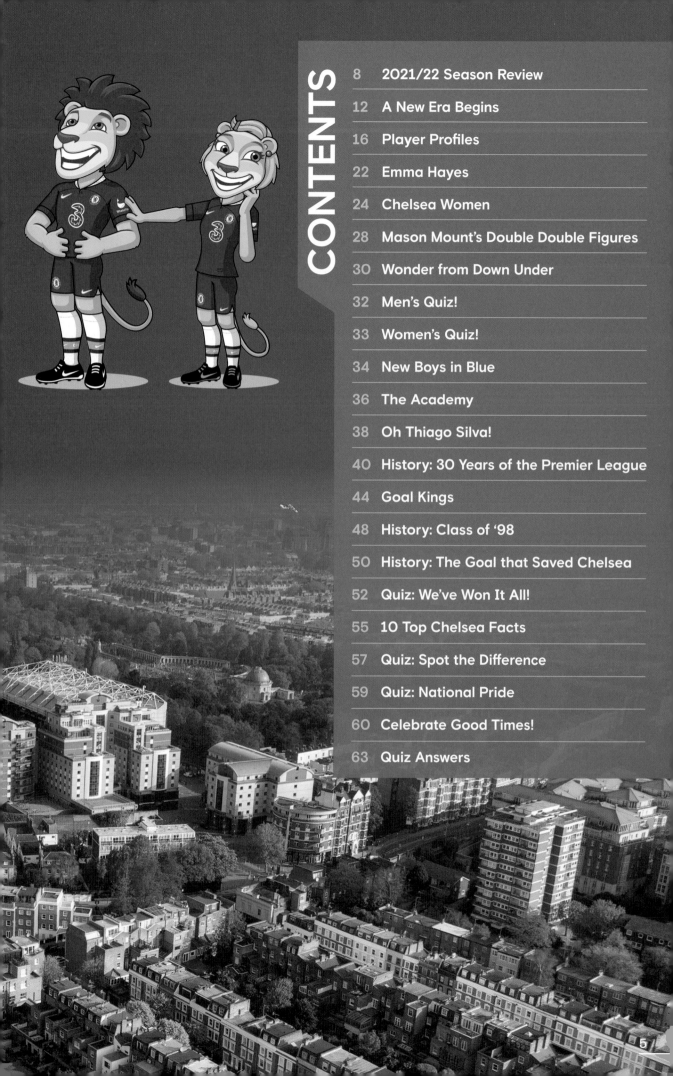

CONTENTS

LONDON'S FINEST

THIS IS O

THE PRIDE

The dressing room is a sacred place, off limits to all but a select few. Before anyone arrives on a matchday it's serenity personified, but the message is clear as soon as the players arrive: this is about more than just the 90 minutes ahead of you. We are the Pride of London and Stamford Bridge is our home – go out there and show what it means to be Chelsea.

It was another intense campaign for Chelsea as we played 63 games in all competitions, before ending with two trophies to our name and two painfully close cup-final defeats. We take a look at the season in which we completed the set of major trophies and became...

CHAMPIONS OF THE WORLD

THE FIFA CLUB WORLD CUP TROPHY

We began the season with the UEFA Super Cup against Europa League winners Villarreal, of Spain, which took place in Belfast. Following a tense 1–1 draw, we won the game on a penalty shootout after Kepa Arrizabalaga came on especially for spot kicks.

Ahead of the first game of our Champions League defence in September, UEFA handed out awards to four Chelsea men for their performances when we won the competition the season before. Edouard Mendy was

Our biggest victory of the season was a massive 7-0 win over Norwich City at the Bridge in October. Mason Mount scored his first senior hat-trick in the game.

One of our most complete performances of the season was a 4-0 win at home to Juventus in the Champions League group stage. Three of our goalscorers that night had come through the Chelsea Academy – Trevoh Chalobah, Reece James and Callum Hudson-Odoi. The fourth was scored by Timo Werner.

named Champions League Goalkeeper of the Season, Thomas Tuchel won Men's Coach of the Year, Jorginho was Men's Player of the Year and N'Golo Kante received the Champions League Midfielder of the Season prize.

Before September was out, we had won away at both our north London rivals, beating Arsenal in the second game of the season, then putting Spurs to the sword 3-0 the following month. It's fair to say Thiago Silva was happy with his opening goal at Tottenham!

Things didn't go very well for Chelsea in December and we lost ground in the title ⊙→

WE BEAT NORWICH 7-0!!!

CHAMPIONS

FIFA CLUB WORLD CUP UAE 2021™ PRESENTED BY ⊖ Alibaba Cloud

NOW BLUES FANS COULD SING "WE'VE WON IT ALL!" AND NO ONE COULD ARGUE

race. However, we began 2022 with one of the games of the season as we came from two goals down to draw 2-2 with Liverpool. Mateo Kovacic's amazing volley in that game was later named Chelsea's Goal of the Season.

Kova had competition for that prize, though, when Hakim Ziyech scored an absolute pearler in our home win against Tottenham later that same month. It was one of four victories over Spurs in all competitions – as we beat them in both legs of our Carabao Cup semi-final as well – without conceding a goal.

In February, we took a break from our domestic season to compete in the FIFA Club World Cup in Abu Dhabi. After beating Al-Hilal of Saudi Arabia in the semi-finals, we met Brazilian club Palmeiras in the final, and won thanks to an extra-time penalty from Kai Havertz. Scoring the winner in the previous season's Champions League final had made sure he would go down in Chelsea history,

KOVA'S GOAL OF THE SEASON!

now he had secured the last missing trophy from our collection. Now Blues fans could sing "We've won it all!" and no one could argue.

Sadly we had less luck in the Carabao Cup final against Liverpool at Wembley. A great game, with chances at both ends, somehow ended 0-0 and went to a penalty shootout. After an incredible 21 successful spot kicks in a row, our sub goalkeeper Kepa stepped up to take the 22nd and missed. He had been

the hero in the Super Cup, but this time it just didn't work out.

The Champions League knockout rounds returned and we defeated Lille in the last 16 to set up a quarter-final against Real Madrid. After a poor first leg, which we lost 3-1 at Stamford Bridge, we trounced Southampton 6-0 in the league and our confidence was restored ahead of the second leg. Incredibly, we scored three times without reply in Madrid and took the lead in the tie, only for them to equalise late on and take the game to extra time, where Real ran out winners. Our Champions League defence was over but we'd been so close to turning things around.

Thomas Tuchel continued his fantastic record of guiding us to finals as we beat Crystal Palace 2-0 in the FA Cup semi-final

at Wembley. Ruben Loftus-Cheek came off the bench to break the deadlock, before Mason Mount doubled our lead and secured our progress to the final, where Liverpool once again awaited us.

Sadly, there was heartbreak at Wembley in the FA Cup final. Once again, we played out a thrilling 0-0 draw with Liverpool, as each team missed golden chances to win it in normal time, before losing on penalties, just as we had done in the Carabao Cup. However, we secured third place in the Premier League and Champions League football in our final games of the season to ensure that we finished on a positive note.

Chelsea fans voted for Mason Mount as their Player of the Year, and he picked up the award after our final game of the campaign, against Watford at the Bridge, before the players did a lap of appreciation for the supporters after a long, hard season of 63 games!

ALWAYS FUN BEATING SPURS!

A NEW ERA BEGINS

José E. Feliciano, Behdad Eghbali and Todd Boehly watch a training session during our pre-season trip to Los Angeles

For the first time in almost two decades, Chelsea Football Club has changed hands! Here's what you need to know about our new ownership group, along with a brief history of those who have previously owned the club...

In March 2022, Roman Abramovich announced his intention to sell Chelsea Football Club after 19 successful years of ownership. However, a few days later, the club was sanctioned by the UK Government, which meant it operated within the confines and constraints of the restrictive General Licence granted by the UK Government, while doing its best to maintain the ordinary course of business.

A transaction such as this would normally take at least nine months to complete, and the club received more than 250 enquiries from proposed purchasers. Twelve were deemed to be credible bids, resulting in four and then three final bidders before the Todd Boehly and Clearlake Capital consortium was chosen as the preferred bidder. The transaction was completed only 85 days after the club was put up for sale.

Boehly was named as the new chairman of the club, but there are plenty of other names for you to become acquainted with after the board of directors were confirmed:

Behdad Eghbali and José E. Feliciano are co-controlling owners of Chelsea FC, and co-founders and managing partners of Clearlake Capital.

Mark Walter, co-owner of Chelsea FC, co-founder and CEO of Guggenheim Partners and, along with Boehly, owner of Los Angeles Dodgers, Los Angeles Lakers, and Los Angeles Sparks.

Hansjörg Wyss, co-owner of Chelsea FC, founder of the Wyss Foundation.

Jonathan Goldstein, co-owner of Chelsea FC, co-founder and CEO of Cain International.

Barbara Charone, director and co-founder of MBC PR.

Lord Daniel Finkelstein OBE, columnist and former executive editor of The Times.

James Pade, partner and managing director of Clearlake Capital.

"WE ARE HONOURED TO BECOME THE NEW CUSTODIANS OF CHELSEA FOOTBALL CLUB. WE'RE ALL IN – 100 PER CENT – EVERY MINUTE OF EVERY MATCH. OUR VISION AS OWNERS IS CLEAR: WE WANT TO MAKE THE FANS PROUD. ALONG WITH OUR COMMITMENT TO DEVELOPING THE YOUTH SQUAD AND ACQUIRING THE BEST TALENT, OUR PLAN OF ACTION IS TO INVEST IN THE CLUB FOR THE LONG–TERM AND BUILD ON CHELSEA'S REMARKABLE HISTORY OF SUCCESS."

OUR HISTORY **OF OWNERS**

1905-1980

THE MEARS FAMILY

The majority of Chelsea's history has been under the ownership of the Mears family. On 10 March 1905, there was a meeting in the Rising Sun pub – today called the Butcher's Hook – opposite Stamford Bridge to discuss a new football club to play at a stadium that was, at the time, primarily used for athletics. The Bridge was owned by brothers Gus and Joseph Mears, who pushed ahead with the plans to form Chelsea Football Club along with a few other key figures. The rest, as they say, is history – and the Mearses dominated the boardroom for the best part of eight decades. Although Gus passed away a few years after the club's formation, Joseph continued to lead the club before the baton was passed to his son, Joe, and then his grandson, Brian. It was under the stewardship of the latter that a huge redevelopment of Stamford Bridge was planned, which almost sent the club under...

1982-2003

KEN BATES

In the latter years of the Mears era, property developers had gained ownership of our stadium's land and the club was in turmoil. In stepped Ken Bates, who had been on the board at Football League clubs in Lancashire, and in April 1982 he famously purchased Chelsea Football Club for the princely sum of £1! But that didn't include Stamford Bridge, and so the biggest battle of his tenure was to save the Bridge. He managed to do just that, with the many supporters who pledged money to the cause becoming the Chelsea Pitch Owners (CPO), which divides the ownership of the land the stadium sits on among many thousands. Bates then set about awakening a sleeping giant, as the stadium was redeveloped and stars of world football were signed up, bringing the good times back to the club. We won major silverware for the first time in decades and played Champions League football for the first time, making this a fondly remembered era in west London.

2003-2022

ROMAN ABRAMOVICH

On 1 July 2003, Russian businessman Roman Abramovich bought the club from Bates and kickstarted a new era of unprecedented success at Stamford Bridge. With the same burning ambition and vision for the big time that characterised Chelsea at our birth nearly 100 years earlier, the new owner quickly set about clearing all debt, and that summer he made – at that point – the biggest outlay on players in British football history. Soon, the trophies began flooding in. We became champions of England for the first time in 50 years and domestically we won the lot before finally lifting the Champions League for the first time in 2012, becoming kings of Europe. Chelsea were among the very best sides in the world – and the same could be said of our Women's team and the Academy – and during the 19 years of the Abramovich era, we won it all. That fact was confirmed in the final days of the Russian's tenure, as we won the Club World Cup for the first time.

BEN CHILWELL

RAHEEM STERLING

CHELSEA FOOTBALL CLUB

THE SHED END

PLAYER PROFILES

*All stats correct ahead of the 2022/23 season.

KEPA
ARRIZABALAGA

Position:	Goalkeeper
Date of birth:	03.10.1994
Nationality:	Spanish
Signed from:	Athletic Bilbao (August 2018)
Appearances:	124
Clean sheets:	46

DID YOU KNOW?

Kepa came off the bench especially for penalty shootouts twice last season. We won one of those, against Villarreal in the Super Cup, but lost the other, in the Carabao Cup final against Liverpool.

MARCUS
BETTINELLI

Position:	Goalkeeper
Date of birth:	24.05.1992
Nationality:	English
Signed from:	Fulham (July 2021)
Appearances:	1
Clean sheets:	0

DID YOU KNOW?

Bettinelli made his only Chelsea appearance to date in our FA Cup third round victory over Chesterfield at Stamford Bridge last season.

EDOUARD
MENDY

Position:	Goalkeeper
Date of birth:	01.03.1992
Nationality:	Senegalese
Signed from:	Rennes (September 2020)
Appearances:	93
Clean sheets:	48

DID YOU KNOW?

Mendy won the Africa Cup of Nations with Senegal in the middle of last season, and also helped his country to qualify for the World Cup. On both occasions they beat Egypt on penalties!

CESAR
AZPILICUETA

Position:	Defender
Date of birth:	28.08.1989
Nationality:	Spanish
Signed from:	Marseille (August 2012)
Appearances:	476
Goals:	17

DID YOU KNOW?

Azpi has captained Chelsea in over 200 games, after reaching that milestone in April 2022. John Terry holds the record for most games as captain, having worn the armband for the Blues 580 times.

TREVOH
CHALOBAH

Position:	Defender
Date of birth:	05.07.1999
Nationality:	English
Signed from:	Chelsea Academy (July 2016)
Appearances:	30
Goals:	4

DID YOU KNOW?

Chalobah won a trophy on his first-team debut for Chelsea in last season's UEFA Super Cup. He then scored on his home debut against Crystal Palace in his first Premier League game!

BEN
CHILWELL

Position:	Defender
Date of birth:	21.12.1996
Nationality:	English
Signed from:	Leicester City (August 2020)
Appearances:	55
Goals:	7

DID YOU KNOW?

Ben Chilwell scored in four consecutive Premier League games last season, becoming the first English player to achieve this for Chelsea since Frank Lampard in 2013.

MARC
CUCURELLA

Position:	Defender
Date of birth:	22.07.1998
Nationality:	Spanish
Signed from:	Brighton & Hove Albion (August 2022)
Appearances:	0
Goals:	0

DID YOU KNOW?

Cucurella began his career as a youngster with Barcelona and has represented Spain since Under-16s level.

WESLEY
FOFANA

Position:	Defender
Date of birth:	17.12.2000
Nationality:	French
Signed from:	Leicester City (August 2022)
Azppearances:	0
Goals:	0

DID YOU KNOW?

Fofana was part of the Leicester City team that beat us in the FA Cup final at Wembley in 2021, for which he claimed his first winners' medal in club football.

REECE
JAMES

Position:	Defender
Date of birth:	08.12.1999
Nationality:	English
Signed from:	Chelsea Academy (March 2017)
Appearances:	123
Goals:	9

DID YOU KNOW?

Reece's dad, Nigel, is a football coach and a former professional player himself. No wonder Reece and Lauren ended up playing for Chelsea!

KALIDOU
KOULIBALY

Position:	Defender
Date of birth:	20.06.1991
Nationality:	Senegalese
Signed from:	Napoli (July 2022)
Appearances:	0
Goals:	0

DID YOU KNOW?

Koulibaly was a team-mate of Jorginho's at Napoli and plays international football alongside Edou Mendy for Senegal, so he had some good friends to introduce him to Chelsea!

THIAGO
SILVA

Position:	Defender
Date of birth:	22.09.1984
Nationality:	Brazilian
Signed from:	Paris Saint-Germain (August 2020)
Appearances:	82
Goals:	5

DID YOU KNOW?

In April 2022, Thiago Silva became the oldest outfield player ever to appear for Chelsea in the Premier League, aged 37 years and 210 days. He is also our oldest Premier League goalscorer.

CARNEY
CHUKWUEMEKA

Position:	Midfielder
Date of birth:	20.10.2003
Nationality:	English
Signed from:	Aston Villa (August 2022)
Appearances:	0
Goals:	0

DID YOU KNOW?

Carney was part of the young England squad that won the European Under-19 Championship last summer, scoring in the final against Israel.

CONOR
GALLAGHER

Position:	Midfielder
Date of birth:	06.02.2000
Nationality:	English
Signed from:	Chelsea Academy (March 2017)
Appearances:	0
Goals:	0

DID YOU KNOW?

Gallagher won Crystal Palace's Player of the Year award last season while on loan there, and was named West Bromwich Albion's Young Player of the Year during his previous loan.

JORGINHO

Position:	Midfielder
Date of birth:	20.12.1991
Nationality:	Italian
Signed from:	Napoli (July 2018)
Appearances:	188
Goals:	26

N'GOLO
KANTE

Position:	Midfielder
Date of birth:	29.03.1991
Nationality:	French
Signed from:	Leicester City (July 2016)
Appearances:	260
Goals:	13

MATEO
KOVACIC

Position:	Midfielder
Date of birth:	06.05.1994
Nationality:	Croatian
Signed from:	Real Madrid (July 2019)
Appearances:	184
Goals:	4

RUBEN
LOFTUS-CHEEK

Position:	Midfielder
Date of birth:	23.01.1996
Nationality:	English
Signed from:	Chelsea Academy (January 2013)
Appearances:	122
Goals:	13

MASON
MOUNT

Position:	Midfielder
Date of birth:	10.01.1999
Nationality:	English
Signed from:	Chelsea Academy (January 2016)
Appearances:	160
Goals:	30

DENIS
ZAKARIA

Position:	Midfielder
Date of birth:	20.11.1996
Nationality:	Swiss
Signed from:	Juventus (season-long loan)
Appearances:	0
Goals:	0

CHRISTIAN
PULISIC

Position:	Midfielder/Forward
Date of birth:	18.09.1998
Nationality:	American
Signed from:	Borussia Dortmund (January 2019)
Appearances:	115
Goals:	25

HAKIM
ZIYECH

Position:	Midfielder/Forward
Date of birth:	19.03.1993
Nationality:	Moroccan
Signed from:	Ajax (July 2020)
Appearances:	83
Goals:	14

PIERRE-EMERICK
AUBAMEYANG

Position:	Forward
Date of birth:	18.06.1989
Nationality:	Gabonese
Signed from:	Barcelona (September 2022)
Appearances:	0
Goals:	0

ARMANDO
BROJA

Position:	Forward
Date of birth:	10.09.2001
Nationality:	English
Signed from:	Chelsea Academy (January 2020)
Appearances:	1
Goals:	0

KAI
HAVERTZ

Position:	Forward
Date of birth:	11.06.1999
Nationality:	German
Signed from:	Bayer Leverkusen (September 2020)
Appearances:	92
Goals:	23

DID YOU KNOW?

Havertz scored the goal that made us champions of Europe in 2021 and then put away the penalty that made us champions of the world last season.

RAHEEM
STERLING

Position:	Forward
Date of birth:	08.12.1994
Nationality:	English
Signed from:	Manchester City (July 2022)
Appearances:	0
Goals:	0

DID YOU KNOW?

Although his previous two clubs – Manchester City and Liverpool – are both in the north of England, Sterling grew up in north-west London, within earshot of Wembley Stadium.

HAYSEY'S AT THE WHEEL!

EMMA HAYES took charge of Chelsea Women for the first time in August 2012 – and since then the club has enjoyed more success than we could have ever dreamed of. This is the lowdown on the charismatic Blues boss...

FOOTY MAD

Hayes was born and raised in Camden, north London, and from a young age it was apparent that she was destined for a career in football. At first that seemed to be on the playing side, as she was part of Arsenal's Academy – but then an ankle injury on a skiing trip put paid to her hopes of ever making it in the game.

Instead of sitting around sulking, Hayes went to university and specialised in European studies, Spanish and sociology, while also taking her coaching badges. She headed for the USA, where women's football was booming, and in 2001, at the age of 25, she became the youngest coach in the league's history.

After coming back to England to work at Arsenal, where she was assistant manager in the year when they became the first, and only, European champions from these shores, Hayes returned to the States for another lengthy stint. It wasn't until 2012 that she took on the formidable task of transforming the fortunes of Chelsea.

BUILDING FROM THE BOTTOM

Although the Blues had reached the Women's FA Cup final under previous manager Matt Beard in 2012, that was exceeding the odds – the club were struggling in the WSL and we had never lifted a major trophy.

Although the England boss at the time was Hope Powell, female managers were few and far between at the top level, but Chelsea gave our backing to Hayes and after a year or so of rebuilding, we began to challenge for major honours.

Proven winners like Katie Chapman were convinced to join a club with no previous record of success, while future legends like Ji So-Yun were tempted by Hayes. The brief was clear: here's your chance to write history at one of the world's biggest football clubs. And, well, you know the next part of the story – since our first silverware was won in 2015, the trophy cabinet has been well stocked ever since!

HONOURED BY ROYALTY
While the team honours, not to mention the personal awards, have flowed steadily for Hayes, she's also been made an MBE and an OBE by the Queen! That doesn't happen to just anyone, and she was truly moved on both occasions. "It was a huge shock to hear I had been awarded an OBE," she said of her most recent distinction. "It's an unbelievable honour for me and my family and a privilege I take very seriously."

HALL OF FAMER
Whatever happens from here, Hayes is guaranteed her place among the greats of women's football – she's already been inducted into the WSL's Hall of Fame! After she was told the news, Hayes said: "A big motivator for me, that young men, young boys like my son, grow up where they see women in positions I'm in and that's just the norm for them." Her son, Harry, was born in 2018 just a few days after Chelsea won a WSL and FA Cup Double.

VOICE OF REASON
On top of all her coaching success, Hayes has also become one of the more popular pundits on TV after a strong showing during the men's European Championship in 2021. She's also taken the time to get involved in Soccer Aid, where she worked as England's assistant manager alongside Harry Redknapp and Line of Duty star Vicky McClure!

We asked Emma to tell us a bit about what she was like when she was growing up…

KICKABOUTS
I just used to play at the flats with all the boys, and we'd try to get all the girls involved as well. It was always on concrete and sometimes you'd end up with 20-a-side matches. The bigger boys would toe punt the ball as hard as they could at you and you had to pretend it didn't hurt!

FOOTBALL HEROES
The 1986 World Cup blew me away and I instantly became a fan of Argentina. They were led by this little porky fella with curly hair, who couldn't look less like a footballer. I'd stand in front of the telly as a 10-year-old and think, "This is the most amazing thing in the world." Diego Maradona is still the greatest footballer there's ever been, as far as I'm concerned.

I also loved Glenn Hoddle. When I was a kid, my mum and dad had a sweet shop in Covent Garden and Glenn came in one day. I happened to be behind the till and I just couldn't bring myself to take his money! I remember watching Glenn in his prime and thinking, "What country is this player from?" He was so different to any other English player at that time.

FOOTBALL POSITION
No10. I'm left footed and I'm not going to lie to you, defending is not my forte. I'd happily create or score all day, every day, but I can just picture a few of my players now screaming at me to get back!

WHEN I WASN'T PLAYING FOOTBALL
I was being cheeky! But I also loved trying to build or create something, whether it was a go kart, helping to construct something with Lego, whatever. And if I wasn't doing that or playing football, I used to just run around the estate. My mum used to call me a street urchin!

CHELSEA WOMEN

The Chelsea Women success story continues to produce chapter after chapter, following another incredible year in which the Blues added more major silverware to the trophy cabinet...

HAT-TRICK OF TITLES

The Blues made WSL history in the 2021/22 campaign, as for the first-time ever a team won the title three years on the trot! We were trailing Arsenal for much of the campaign after losing to the Gunners on the opening day of the season, but Emma Hayes' side never know when they're beaten and an incredible run in the new year took us all the way to a WSL hat-trick. A final-day win over Manchester United after we had twice trailed to the Red Devils was a thrilling way to seal the title!

FA CUP DOUBLE

It wasn't just in the league that we rewrote the history books! We went to Wembley twice for the Women's FA Cup final – once in December, as the 2020/21 competition had been delayed due to Covid-19, and again in May to close out the last campaign. In the first, Sam Kerr's sumptuous chip helped us to see off Arsenal, and we had our hands on the trophy again a few months later when the Australian scored one more at the home of English football to beat Manchester City. That game is probably better remembered for Erin Cuthbert's Wembley wonder strike, which is right up there with Kerr's chip as one of the best-ever FA Cup final goals!

WE WENT TO WEMBLEY TWICE FOR THE WOMEN'S FA CUP FINAL – ONCE IN DECEMBER, AS THE 2020/21 COMPETITION HAD BEEN DELAYED DUE TO COVID-19

EURO GLORY

Chelsea Women played a big part in England's first-ever major trophy as four of our players helped the Lionesses win Euro 2022! Millie Bright and Fran Kirby started every game at the tournament, while Jess Carter and Bethany England were also part of the squad, as history was made! Here's what our winning quartet had to say about it...

"I hope everyone is proud of what this nation has achieved, not just us winning, but the crowds we have rallied up game after game. The women's game is massive now. It's to be respected. This is the foundation and we have to move on from this in the WSL and other leagues. We set the tone and now we need to keep it going."

MILLIE BRIGHT

"It's something that I've dreamed of for a long time. I failed a couple of times with this team so to win this now is amazing. It's incredible. I got to the 2015 World Cup and we've been at a few semi-finals since then, so to get to the final and win this one is amazing."

FRAN KIRBY

"I've got very few words besides it's a bit mad, really! The whole thing has been a journey, it's been tough, but the winning moment has made it worth it. In the dressing room afterwards, we had a lot of beers, a lot of food, and a lot of awful dancing and singing!"

JESS CARTER

"I'm so proud to have been a part of this amazing, history-making group. Thank you to my friends and family who supported me throughout and a special thanks goes to the record-breaking number of you who got behind us at Wembley Stadium – we couldn't have done it without you!"

BETHANY ENGLAND

GOLD STANDARD

Chelsea Women once again dominated the individual WSL awards in 2021/22. For the third season in a row, and fifth time overall,

Emma Hayes was named Manager of the Year. No one else has won it more than once! Sam Kerr's wonder strike on the final day against Manchester United won her Goal of the Season and she was also named WSL Player of the Year, following in the footsteps of Fran Kirby and Bethany England in the previous two seasons. That wasn't all for Kerr, as she was also chosen as the best women's footballer in the country by the Professional Footballers' Association (PFA) and Football Writers' Association (FWA). What a season she had!

COVER STAR

Sam Kerr is making history as the first female player to appear on the global cover of EA Sports' FIFA game series! Previously,

female footballers have only appeared on regional covers – America's Alex Morgan and Canada's Christine Sinclair were alongside Lionel Messi for the North American edition of FIFA 16. Kerr is joined by Paris Saint-Germain and France striker Kylian Mbappe on the cover of FIFA 23 Ultimate Edition and, for the first time ever, FA Women's Super League teams will appear in the game!

LEGENDS BOW OUT

On the final day of the 2021/22 WSL season at Kingsmeadow, there was barely a dry eye in the house, despite the Blues having just claimed the league title for the third year in a row. The tears were for three legendary figures who were turning out at our home ground for the last time as Chelsea players. Drew Spence had been here since 2008, when the club

was a million miles from the one she was leaving behind; Ji So-Yun, in the words of Emma Hayes, "the best international player in WSL history"; and Jonna Andersson was the understated Swedish left-back who diligently went about her business in three Double-winning sides. The three of them will always be welcome back at Kingsmeadow.

ONE TEAM, ONE DREAM

If you've ever wondered what happens behind the scenes at Chelsea Women, you really need to watch One Team, One Dream. This documentary series follows the fortunes of the Blues between 2019 and 2021 and it features unprecedented 24/7 access to the home ground, training sessions, team bus, dressing room, and wherever the season takes them, as well as following the players' home lives. You can catch it all on DAZN or on DAZN's YouTube channel.

MEET THE
NEW SIGNINGS

It was a busy summer in the transfer market ahead of the 2022/23 season. Here's a little bit about each of the new signings who came into the club…

KADEISHA
BUCHANAN

Five Champions League triumphs with Lyon highlights the level this centre-half has maintained since moving to Europe. Incredibly, she began her international career with Canada at the age of 14 and has won her country's Player of the Year award three times.

EVE
PERISSET

Like Buchanan, Perisset was playing in the French league before coming to Chelsea as she was with Bordeaux in her homeland. Blues fans were certainly impressed with what they saw from this exciting full-back, who can also play in midfield, as she starred for France at the Euros.

KATERINA
SVITKOVA

We'd come up against this exciting attacking midfielder during her two years with West Ham United in the WSL – in fact, she has a goal against Chelsea to her name after netting in last season's Continental League Cup tie between the sides!

JELENA
CANKOVIC

Hayes reckons we've added a significant layer of creativity to our midfield with the addition of the Serbian international, who seems born to win league titles. She has played in four different countries during her career and won a championship in each of them!

JOHANNA
RYTTING KANERYD

JRK won the league title in Sweden with Rosengard, before going on to become one of the league's stars with BK Hacken. She's got pace to burn and is extremely direct – exactly the type of player to get bums off seats at Kingsmeadow!

MASON MOUNT'S
DOUBLE DOUBLE
FIGURES

The England midfielder was named Player of the Year by Chelsea fans and no wonder after he became only the fifth Blues player in the Premier League era to hit double figures for both goals and assists in a single season.

"I ALWAYS FOCUS IN ON WHERE I CAN IMPROVE"

Mason Mount joined Frank Lampard, Didier Drogba, Juan Mata and Eden Hazard in the very small group of Chelsea players to have reached double figures for both goals and assists in a Premier League season during his dazzling 2021/22 campaign.

The Blues' Player of the Year hit that target when he set up Christian Pulisic for his goal in our 3-0 win against Leeds United in May, three games from the end of the campaign. Earlier in the match he scored one of his best goals yet with a rifled effort into the top corner from the edge of the area. It meant he finished last season with 11 goals and 10 assists to his name in the Premier League alone.

OUR PLAYER OF THE YEAR!

MASON'S PL GOALS 2021/22 (11)

Date	Opposition	Goals
23.10.21	Norwich (h)	3
01.12.21	Watford (a)	1
04.12.21	West Ham (a)	1
11.12.21	Leeds (h)	1
16.12.21	Everton (h)	1
10.03.22	Norwich (a)	1
09.04.22	Southampton (a)	2
11.05.22	Leeds (a)	1

MASON'S PL ASSISTS 2021/22 (10)

Date	Opposition	Scorer
22.08.21	Arsenal (a)	Reece James
23.10.21	Norwich (h)	Reece James
01.12.21	Watford (a)	Hakim Ziyech
04.12.21	West Ham (a)	Thiago Silva
29.12.21	Brighton (h)	Romelu Lukaku
23.01.22	Tottenham (h)	Thiago Silva
10.03.22	Norwich (a)	Trevoh Chalobah
09.04.22	Southampton (a)	Marcos Alonso
20.04.22	Arsenal (h)	Cesar Azpilicueta
11.05.22	Leeds (a)	Christian Pulisic

In all competitions, he totalled 13 goals and 16 assists.

"I was buzzing to reach that target," he said in an interview with the matchday programme. "It's a massive focus of mine when I set goals at the beginning of a season. I've always looked to get double figures in both, which is obviously very difficult, so I'm pleased.

"I always focus in on where I can improve, which is the assists side, because I've naturally got goals in me. If I can get forward and arrive later into the box, as a midfielder, I feel like I can score goals, if I'm working in training on the techniques as well.

"Assists can be a bit harder at times. It helps when you take set-pieces because it's a big part of the game. You always see people asking about set-pieces, if it's an assist or not, but when you put the ball in the right position for your team-mate to score then it's an assist. How many goals are scored from set-pieces? It's massive and it can have a big effect on the game, so I've focused on that and then just tried to add more assists as well."

WONDER FROM DOWN UNDER

SAM KERR simply hasn't stopped scoring goals since she joined Chelsea midway through the 2019/20 season. This is why the prolific Australian is already assured of legend status at Kingsmeadow...

Sam Kerr is a centre-back's nightmare. As a striker, she's got just about everything needed to lead the line in any system. She's quick, strong, capable of finishing with either foot or her head, and she's got the trait that any football manager will tell you is nigh on impossible to coach – that innate ability to sniff out a chance.

On top of all that, however, she has the confidence or courage, whatever you want to call it, to keep coming back for more when things aren't going her way. Whether she's spurned one chance or three, if another comes along you can be sure she'll treat it as if nothing happened before. For a centre-back who thinks they're winning the battle, that is a frightening prospect.

When it comes to regularly sticking the ball in the back of the net, there are few better than Kerr currently plying their trade in world football, let alone the Women's Super League. She won the WSL Golden Boot for 2020/21 after scoring 21 times from only 22 appearances and she retained the trophy last term by hitting 20 goals from 20 matches.

None of this is anything new, however, for the Blues No20. She's previously finished as top scorer in the USA and Australia, making her the first player to ever win the Golden Boot across three different leagues, in three different continents. On top of that, she's also the highest-scoring Australian international of all time. What a player!

FENOMENO FAN

Sam's favourite player when she was growing up is an all-time great of the game: the Brazilian centre-forward Ronaldo, known in his homeland as O Fenomeno, which means The Phenomenon. Just watch his YouTube highlights reel to find out why! "I liked his flair and the way he played the game," says Sam. "He played with no care and it looked like he was having fun out there."

FACTFILE:

Position: **Forward**
Date of birth: **10.09.93**
Nationality: **Australian**
Signed from:
Chicago Red Stars (December 2019)
CFC apps: **78**
CFC goals: **61**

* Stats correct up to end of 2021/22 season

FINAL SPECIALIST

Due to the 2020/21 Women's FA Cup final being delayed until midway through the next campaign, Kerr was able to record a unique achievement – she scored in two FA Cup finals in the same season! Not only that, but she scored twice in each final, as we beat Arsenal and Manchester City to lift the trophy twice in the space of six months. Her goals tally for Chelsea in major finals now stands at eight in six games, which even Didier Drogba – long regarded as the club's greatest big-game player – can only dream of!

AUSSIE RULES

Believe it or not, Kerr didn't get into football properly until she was 15. "I used to play Aussie rules, but my mum and dad stopped me from playing after I started coming home with black eyes and a bloodied face," she said of a sport that makes rugby look like a stroll in the park. We think her parents made the right call there...

AWARD TOUR

Kerr's 2021/22 season wasn't just filled with major honours with the Blues – she swept the board of individual awards in English football. Chelsea supporters, the PFA, the Football Writers' Association and the WSL all chose her as Player of the Year, while her incredible lob against Manchester United on the final day was also selected as the WSL's Goal of the Season. On top of that, she also finished third in the Ballon d'Or voting midway through the campaign.

FLIPPING BRILLIANT

In the summer of 2020, ahead of Australia being announced as co-hosts of the next Women's World Cup, an image of Sam doing her trademark backflip celebration was projected onto the Sydney Opera House! How many footballers can say that?!

GETTING TO KNOW YOU

Here's a few quick-fire questions with Sam to find out what she's like off the pitch...

My team-mates would describe me as...
funny, a class clown and a good team player.

My favourite food is...
sushi.

The traditional English food I like is...
cottage pie and a roast dinner.

My coffee order is...
a latte.

My pets are...
a dog at home in Australia called Billie. I have a cat here and she's called Helen.

My favourite movie is...
Law Abiding Citizen.

If I was a superhero my power would be...
invisibility. That's easy!

You'd never guess...
I have a fear of flying, I'm literally terrible at flying, it's by far my biggest fear.

EMMA ON SAM KERR:

"Champions don't make excuses or look for anybody else to manage them. Sam takes responsibility and every time I listen to her and every time I watch her perform, she's in charge. She's in control of making sure that she sets the standards for herself and that's what I admire about her. She sets that tone in such a way that I've rarely seen."

CHELSEA MEN'S
QUIZ!

How much do you know about the current Chelsea men's team players?
We've put together 10 tricky questions to test your Blues knowledge!

1 We won last season's FIFA Club World Cup with a late penalty in extra time, but who took it?

2 The World Cup falls in the middle of the 2022/23 season, but who is the only current Chelsea player to have won it?

3 How many Chelsea goals did Mason Mount score in all competitions in the 2021/22 season?

○ a) 10   ○ b) 13   ○ c) 16

4 Our Champions League title defence ended in defeat to Real Madrid at the quarter-final stage last season, but which club did we beat in the last 16?

5 Which member of our men's team has a sister called Lauren who plays for Chelsea Women?

6 Blues keeper Edouard Mendy won the Africa Cup of Nations in February 2022, but which national team was he representing?

7 Against which London club did Trevoh Chalobah score on his Premier League debut for Chelsea in August 2021?

8 Which Chelsea player's grandfather represented the England amateur national team in 1949?

○ a) Ben Chilwell   ○ b) Mason Mount   ○ c) Reece James

9 At which French club did Thomas Tuchel coach Thiago Silva before they both moved to Stamford Bridge?

10 Mateo Kovacic scored Chelsea's Goal of the Season for 2021/22, but who were our opponents in that thrilling game at the Bridge?

Answers on p63

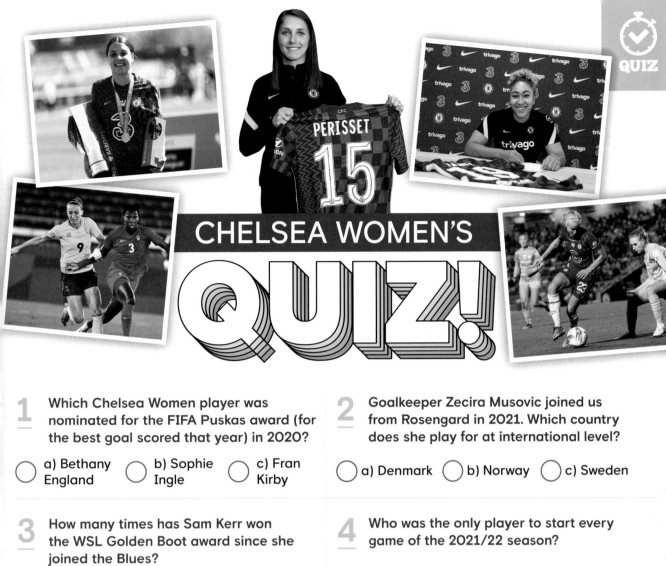

CHELSEA WOMEN'S QUIZ!

1 Which Chelsea Women player was nominated for the FIFA Puskas award (for the best goal scored that year) in 2020?

- a) Bethany England
- b) Sophie Ingle
- c) Fran Kirby

2 Goalkeeper Zecira Musovic joined us from Rosengard in 2021. Which country does she play for at international level?

- a) Denmark
- b) Norway
- c) Sweden

3 How many times has Sam Kerr won the WSL Golden Boot award since she joined the Blues?

- a) One
- b) Two
- c) Three

4 Who was the only player to start every game of the 2021/22 season?

- a) Millie Bright
- b) Jess Carter
- c) Magda Eriksson

5 From which of our fellow WSL clubs did we sign Lauren James in the summer of 2021?

- a) Arsenal
- b) Leicester City
- c) Man United

6 Kadeisha Buchanan joined us from Lyon, but which of her Chelsea team-mates does she also play with for Canada?

- a) Jessie Fleming
- b) Pernille Harder
- c) Melanie Leupolz

7 Which number does Fran Kirby wear for the Blues?

- a) 9
- b) 11
- c) 14

8 Who was the only Chelsea midfielder to be named in the 2021/22 PFA WSL Team of the Year?

- a) Ji So-Yun
- b) Guro Reiten
- c) Drew Spence

9 Pernille Harder has spent the past two seasons with Chelsea, but which German club did she play for prior to that?

- a) Bayern Munich
- b) Eintracht Frankfurt
- c) Wolfsburg

10 Eve Perisset is the first player from which country to represent Chelsea?

- a) France
- b) Luxembourg
- c) Switzerland

Answers on p63

NEW BOYS IN BLUE

There was plenty of activity at Stamford Bridge during the summer transfer window. Here's what you need to know about the players hoping to become future Blues heroes...

RAHEEM STERLING

You'll have seen Raz tormenting Premier League defences on his way to winning numerous titles with Manchester City, not to mention his quality performances for England which helped the Three Lions reach the final of the European Championship in 2021.

In fact, there's probably not a lot we can tell you about Sterling that you don't already know, so allow Mason Mount and Reece James, who already knew him well from international duty, to do our job!

"I've been lucky enough to play with Raz for the last couple of years with England," said Mase. "He's scored a lot and he creates a lot because he's dangerous anytime he has the ball – and he's also a massive threat when he doesn't have it.

Reece didn't need as many words to express his joy that Sterling had joined us: "Playing against him is a nightmare so I'm pretty happy that he's here now and I don't need to play against him anymore!"

PIERRE-EMERICK AUBAMEYANG

We know all about the threat posed by Auba from his time with Arsenal, and now the prolific frontman plans to bring those goals to west London following a brief spell with Barcelona.

A pacey striker and clinical finisher, the former Gabon international is a proven Premier League goalscorer having netted 68 times for Arsenal over four years at the Emirates, averaging better than a goal every two games in all competitions and sharing the Golden Boot award in 2018/19 alongside Liverpool duo Sadio Mane and Mohamed Salah.

It seems he still has plenty to prove in England, as he said upon signing for the Blues: "I have some unfinished business with the Premier League, so it's good to be back and really exciting."

KALIDOU KOULIBALY

When Chelsea legends like Didier Drogba, John Terry and Gianfranco Zola text you to say you've made the right choice by joining the club, it's probably a pretty good sign... As one of Serie A's most impressive defenders in recent years during his time with Napoli, along with winning the Africa Cup of Nations alongside Edou Mendy with Senegal, it's fair to say Koulibaly is established as one of the leading central defenders in world football.

He's a natural leader, so it was fitting that he decided to take the No26 shirt that was worn for almost two decades by John Terry, Chelsea's captain, leader, legend. He only did so after having a chat over the phone with our former defender – although not before JT had hung up on him as he thought he was being pranked!

CARNEY CHUKWUEMEKA

Although this midfield all-rounder is still in the early stages of his career, he's already taken big strides in a short space of time. After breaking through with Aston Villa last season, he capped off a fine 2022 by scoring for England in the final of the European Under-19 Championship, a tournament at which he was named in the UEFA Team of the Tournament.

Paul Merson, who is an Arsenal legend but a massive Chelsea fan, watched him for Aston Villa at the start of the 2021/22 campaign and he had no doubts then that Carney is set to reach the very top.

"At 17 years old, you are playing in the Premier League in the centre of midfield – I mean, that's a big ask. He will be an absolute star. He glides across the pitch. He is a nice size. He gets on the ball. He looks for it and makes runs without the ball."

MARC CUCERELLA

Compliments don't come much bigger than being described as "the new Azpi", but it's easy to see why Thomas Tuchel said that after completing the signing of a defender who is comfortable playing as a centre-half in a back three or as a left-sided wing-back or full-back.

Cucerella had only played in the Premier League for a season with Brighton before the Blues decided to bring him in, but he was so impressive for the Seagulls that he won their Player of the Season awards as voted for by both the fans and his team-mates. Only three players made more tackles than him in the last Premier League campaign too!

His football upbringing was impressive, as he joined Barcelona at the age of 14 and was schooled at Camp Nou before moving on to Getafe to gain more first-team experience.

WESLEY FOFANA

World-class French centre-backs and Chelsea go hand in hand, so it should be a match made in heaven for Fofana and his new club after he joined us from Leicester City.

Few people in English football knew much about this prodigiously talented defender when he first set foot in the Premier League with the Foxes in 2020, but by the end of his maiden campaign on these shores he'd become a superstar after helping his club to FA Cup glory – at Chelsea's expense!

Prior to his time at the King Power Stadium, he had played for Saint-Etienne – where he came through the ranks – and he's been capped at Under-21 level by the French national team.

Now that he's here at Stamford Bridge, he's got one thing on his mind: lifting silverware. "I'm here to win trophies – the Champions League, Premier League, FA Cup, Carabao Cup, everything."

DENIS ZAKARIA

At 6ft 3in tall, along with bundles of energy and a fondness for getting stuck in, Zakaria felt like a ready-made Premier League signing when the Blues brought him in on transfer deadline day.

The Swiss international agreed a loan move from Juventus for the 2022/23 campaign, bringing with him experience of both Italy's Serie A and Germany's Bundesliga, where he featured for Borussia Monchengladbach.

On top of that, he gives the manager options; although primarily a defensive midfielder, Zakaria can also play further forward or in central defence. He chips in with goals and has played 40 times for the Swiss national team, including at the 2018 World Cup and the European Championship in 2021.

THE ACADEMY

STEPPING UP

Several players from the Chelsea Academy stepped up to represent the first team over the course of the 2021/22 season, including one who established himself as a regular in the side...

CLEVER TREVOH

When the starting line-up was announced for the UEFA Super Cup game against Villarreal at the start of last season, there was a new name on the team sheet. Not many Blues fans had expected Trevoh Chalobah to be in the team for the big season opener in Belfast, but the Chelsea Academy graduate put in a superb performance at the back as we went on to lift the trophy. The following weekend, he was in the team again for his Premier League debut against Crystal Palace, and he lit up Stamford Bridge with a screamer of a goal to cap off a special day for him and his watching family.

Chalobah, who gained plenty of first-team experience during loan spells with Ipswich Town, Huddersfield Town and French club Lorient before returning to Chelsea, went on to make 30 appearances in 2021/22 and scored four goals, all from centre-back. Apart from that worldie on his Premier League debut, the most memorable was his first in the Champions League, which gave us the lead in a 4-0 win over Juventus at the Bridge.

DID YOU KNOW?

Trevoh's older brother Nathaniel also played for Chelsea after coming through the Academy. He made 15 appearances for us between 2012 and 2017 and now plays for our neighbours Fulham.

GETTING THEIR CHANCE

Three other players from the Chelsea Academy were handed senior debuts by Tuchel last season. Xavier Simons and Jude Soonsup-Bell joined Harvey Vale in the Carabao Cup quarter-final starting line-up at Brentford in December. Simons – a versatile midfield player – stepped in at right wing-back, while Soonsup-Bell played in his favoured position up front with fellow youngster Vale. It was in the striker's role that Soonsup-Bell scored the goal that clinched the Under-18 Premier League Cup for Chelsea as we defeated Fulham 2-1 at Craven Cottage in the final.

Lewis Hall was also called in to join the first-team squad around the turn of the year last season, and got his chance on the left side of our

ALL HAIL VALE

Chelsea's Academy Player of the Season award for last season went to Harvey Vale, whose impressive performances in a creative role behind the striker earned him his first-team debut in December 2021. After starting our Carabao Cup quarter-final win over Brentford, Vale went on to play five times for Thomas Tuchel's team, including three FA Cup games.

Vale also played a big role in our Under-18s, reaching the FA Youth Cup semi-finals and winning the Premier League Cup, while also representing the Under-23s – also known as the development squad – in the Premier League 2 (PL2), the Papa John's Trophy and the UEFA Youth League. He played more league games in the PL2 than any other Chelsea player last season, scoring six times from his No10 position.

"It's a massive privilege to win this award and I'm very grateful," said Harvey after being named Academy Player of the Season. "If you look at some of the players who have won it in the past, they've gone on to do great things for Chelsea and I hope I can do the same."

CAPTAIN MARVEL

Vale capped off a memorable season by captaining England to glory at the European Under-19 Championship in the summer. The Young Lions defeated Israel 3-1 in the final.

Jude Soonsup-Bell

Xavier Simons

Lewis Hall

defence in an FA Cup third round tie against Chesterfield. Hall was one of the stand-out performers at both ends of the pitch as we beat the National League side 5-1, picking out Romelu Lukaku for a debut assist, then seeing his shot parried into the path of Andreas Christensen to head home our fourth.

Several other youngsters were called in to train with the first team, and some were unused substitutes for Tuchel's side. Of course, with the likes of Mason Mount, Reece James, Ruben Loftus-Cheek and Callum Hudson-Odoi for company, they have plenty of other Chelsea youth products to look up to for examples!

OH, THI-A-GO SIL-VA!

"THE PREMIER LEAGUE IS SOMETHING I REALLY WANT TO WIN"

Our Brazilian defender is like Peter Pan – forever young! Even at the age of 38, Thiago Silva is still going strong and last season was one of his best ever. We take a look at what makes him so special.

YOUNG AT HEART

Last season, Thiago Silva became the oldest outfield player to appear for Chelsea in a Premier League game, when he came off the bench against Arsenal at the age of 37 years and 210 days in April. He is now in his third season as a Chelsea player and he hasn't shown any signs of slowing down yet, so what's his secret?

"It's about discipline, especially at my age. Playing at such a high level requires a lot of discipline, from controlling how you eat to how you recover. It's all very important." The fans love him too, and when they sing his name, it gives him more energy.

"As a child, all I wanted to do was play football," he says. "I feel happy to be a reference or an inspiration to other people, for the youngsters that are now starting to play and can look and see how far into their lives they could play – until they are 38 or 39."

DEFENSIVE MASTERCLASS

There is a reason why Thiago Silva is still playing for Chelsea into his late 30s and has over 100 caps for Brazil. He is a smart defender who uses his brain as much as his feet, he always remains calm and he knows exactly what position he needs to be in to halt opposition attacks. He came to English football late after spending most of his career in Brazil, Italy and France, and he studied the Premier League when he first arrived at Chelsea, to make sure that he was ready for it.

"English football is like a mix of all the different leagues," he says. "Here, there's a bit of the French league, a bit of the Brazilian league, a bit of Italy, a bit of Spain. Nobody gives anything away and every team keeps battling for as long as they can keep it up. I really love that because football here is about more than just technique. It feels like hard work can take you a long way here."

NEXT UP: THE PREMIER LEAGUE TITLE!

Despite being one of the best centre-backs of his generation and playing for top clubs like AC Milan and PSG, Thiago Silva had never won the Champions League when he joined Chelsea in 2020. That all changed at the end of his first season as a Blues player, when he got his hands on the biggest trophy of all after our win in the final against Manchester City in Porto.

Even reaching that target wasn't enough to satisfy Thiago Silva, though. He's a born winner and now he wants the Premier League crown.

"It's a dream, something that I crave," he said in Chelsea's matchday programme. "I've won all the national leagues I've played in before, and the Premier League is something I really want to win. That's not discarding the Champions League, or any other competition in any way, but the Premier League is the one I really want to win."

30 YEARS
OF THE PREMIER LEAGUE

In 1992, the top flight of English football was renamed the Premier League and the game in this country has become more and more popular ever since. Chelsea's fortunes have changed more than most in that time, so let's take a look at the Blues' incredible journey over the past three decades of league football...

⃝ DIFFERENT LEAGUE

Until the summer of 1992, the top flight of English football had been known as the First Division and was part of the Football League. That all changed when the Premier League was formed ahead of the 1992/93 season, and the whole way in which the sport was presented changed completely over the years that followed.

So our bruising centre-forward Mick Harford made a little bit of history when he scored in our 1-1 draw with Oldham Athletic on the opening weekend of the season. In doing so, he became Chelsea's first goalscorer of the Premier League era. To give you an idea of how much has changed in the three decades since that result, Oldham now compete in the National League – the fifth tier of English football.

At that time, Chelsea were not one of the title challengers – we had finished 14th in 1992, and didn't finish in the top 10 in the Premier League for another five years.

MICK HARFORD

⃝ HODDLE'S NEW BLUES

Many people believe the first step on the way to a new Chelsea was Glenn Hoddle's arrival as player-manager in 1993. Our mid-table league position didn't change in his three years at Stamford Bridge, but Hoddle did lead us to the FA Cup final in 1994 – where we lost 4-0 to Manchester United – and to the semi-finals of the European Cup Winners' Cup in 1995. In his time in charge, he transformed the way the team trained and prepared for games, bringing modern coaching to Chelsea. He also signed some very exciting players. Mark Hughes was one of the best strikers in Britain at the time he arrived from Manchester United, and Dan Petrescu was a European Cup winner. The biggest name of all was Ruud Gullit, a Ballon d'Or winner and one of the greatest footballers of all time. When he arrived at Chelsea, everything changed, and the whole world began to know our name.

RUUD GULLIT, A BALLON D'OR WINNER

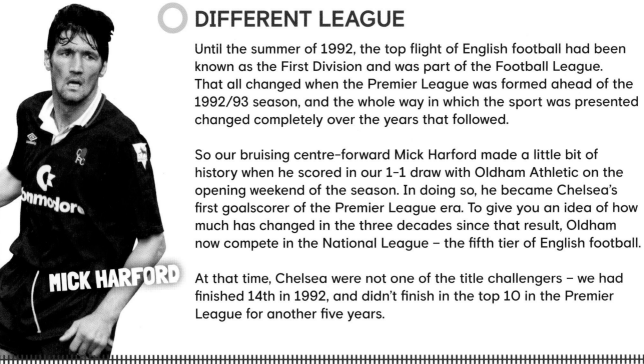

40

THE GLAMOUR YEARS

When Hoddle left to become England manager in 1996, the crowd called for Gullit to take over as Chelsea boss, and they got their wish. The Dutch superstar attracted other famous faces to the club, including Gianluca Vialli, Roberto Di Matteo and Gianfranco Zola. With Londoners like Dennis Wise and Eddie Newton in the team as well, it was a popular side and everyone began to look at what was happening at Stamford Bridge. We finished sixth in 1996/97, and won the FA Cup – our first major trophy for 26 years!

When Gullit left in 1998, Vialli took over as manager and we kept on winning cup competitions, but we couldn't quite crack the Premier League. Our best finish was third in 1998/99, but we did beat Manchester United 5-0 in October 1999, a few months after they had won the Treble. That sent a few shockwaves through English football and Chelsea had become the glamour team.

GIANFRANCO ZOLA GIVES DENNIS WISE A LIFT

CHAMPIONS AT LAST

For the first 11 years of the Premier League, Chelsea were run by chairman Ken Bates, but he sold the club to Roman Abramovich in the summer of 2003. The new owner was a multi-billionaire and was very ambitious – he wanted to win it all for Chelsea and the club spent big to make it happen.

Ahead of his second season, Jose Mourinho was brought in as manager, while Petr Cech and Didier Drogba were among the new players to arrive. They joined a squad led by home-grown captain John Terry and another Londoner, Frank Lampard, the chief goal threat from midfield. Those names are all etched into our history after their generation won trophy after trophy for Chelsea. Our first Premier League title came in 2004/05, and it was sealed with a 2-0 win at Bolton Wanderers, in which Super Frankie Lampard scored both goals. The following year we defended our title to become back-to-back champions of England.

THE DOUBLE

Our third Premier League title, in 2009/10, was extra special because it came as part of our first-ever League and FA Cup Double. By this time, our manager was Carlo Ancelotti, who played ultra-attacking football. We won games 7-2, 7-1, 7-0 and 8-0 that season, the last of which was the result that sealed the league title for us against Wigan Athletic on the final day of the season. We totalled 103 goals that season – the only time we've ever scored more than 100 in the league – and Drogba won the Golden Boot. After winning the FA Cup as well, the team went on an open-top bus tour to celebrate their achievement, as Terry and Lampard joined Ancelotti in singing for the fans who gathered in Eel Brook Common, just down the road from Stamford Bridge.

WE TOTALLED 103 GOALS IN THE 2009/10 DOUBLE WINNING SEASON!

BACK TO THE SUMMIT

Five years passed before Chelsea won the Premier League again, but in the meantime we reached the highest point in the club's history when we became Champions League winners in 2012. The man who brought the league title back to Stamford Bridge 10 years after he had done so for the first time was... Jose Mourinho. Yes, the Portuguese boss returned in 2013 and by 2014/15 he had built a team capable of taking the league by storm, with Cesc Fabregas as the playmaker, Diego Costa as the goalscorer and Eden Hazard providing the magic, while John Terry, Petr Cech and Didier Drogba all picked up their fourth medals in the competition.

Two years later, Antonio Conte built a counter-attacking machine in his favourite 3-4-3 system, and we were champions again. That was the last time we lifted the Premier League trophy, and now we look forward to hailing the next generation of champions.

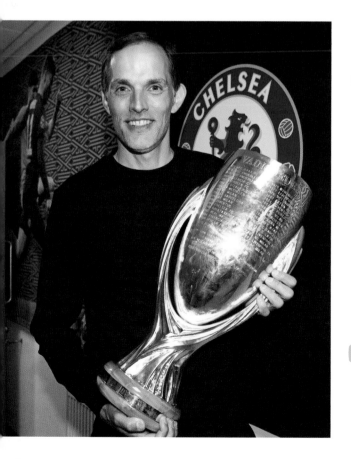

THOMAS TUCHEL

Thomas Tuchel took over as Chelsea manager when Frank Lampard left in January 2021, and by the end of the season he had led us to Champions League glory for the second time in our history. Tuchel also took us to two FA Cup finals and a League Cup final, and won both the UEFA Super Cup and the FIFA Club World Cup.

THOMAS LED US TO SUPER CUP GLORY!

PREMIER LEAGUE
GOAL KINGS

Chelsea have had some prolific scorers over the first 30 years of the Premier League, but do you know which players lead the way when it comes to goals?
Read on to find out...

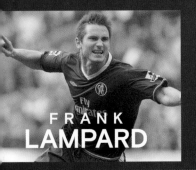

FRANK LAMPARD

It's quite remarkable that a midfielder is in the top six scorers in Premier League history after netting 177 times. All but 30 of those came during his time at Chelsea, when he became our all-time leading scorer and he ripped up the rulebook when it came to what people expected from goalscoring midfielders.

Goals: 147
Apps: 429
CFC career: 2001-14
Best PL season:
22 goals (2009/10)

DIDIER DROGBA

The first African player to score 100 Premier League goals, Drogba was a two-time winner of the Golden Boot, awarded to the league's top scorer. He scored all types of goals, whether tap-ins and headers from inside the box or wonder strikes from distance.

Goals: 104
Apps: 254
CFC career:
2004-12 & 2014-15
Best PL season:
29 goals (2009/10)

EDEN HAZARD

Most people assume the twinkle-toed Belgian was more of a creator than a goalscorer, but he netted 31 times more often than he assisted for the Blues in the Premier League. He famously netted two title-clinching goals – one for Chelsea and then, a year later, to crown Leicester champions at Spurs' expense!

Goals: 85
Apps: 245
CFC career: 2012-19
Best PL season:
16 goals (2016/17 & 2018/19)

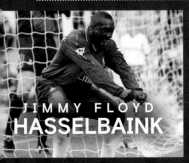

JIMMY FLOYD HASSELBAINK

Chelsea fans had been crying out for a 20-goal-a-season striker since the days of Kerry Dixon. Finally we found one in the destructive Dutchman, who won the Premier League Golden Boot in his first season at the club and just loved scoring against Tottenham.

Goals: 69
Apps: 136
CFC career: 2000-04
Best PL season:
23 goals (2000/01 & 2001/02)

GIANFRANCO ZOLA

Zola was loved by fans throughout the Premier League, always playing the game with a smile on his face and capable of producing magic at any moment. We'd never seen a player quite like him when he joined in 1996 and over the next seven years he brought so much joy – and scored plenty of spectacular goals.

Goals: 147
Apps: 429
CFC career: 1996–03
Best PL season:
14 goals (2002/03)

EIDUR GUDJOHNSEN

Fittingly, the Icelandic striker was an ice-cold finisher in front of goal, most notably in a strike partnership with Hasselbaink in the 2001/02 campaign which remains one of our best ever. His bicycle-kick against Leeds United in 2003 doesn't get talked about enough for our liking!

Goals: 54
Apps: 186
CFC career: 2000–06
Best PL season:
14 goals (2001/02)

DIEGO COSTA

The type of snarling centre-forward who would often be described as a defender's worst nightmare, Diego Costa spearheaded two title-winning Chelsea sides and finished as our top scorer in all three seasons he spent with the club.

Goals: 52
Apps: 89
CFC career: 2014–17
Best PL season:
20 goals (2014/15 & 2016/17)

JOHN TERRY

Although his time at Chelsea spanned the best part of 20 years, it's still some effort for JT to get onto this list considering he was a centre-back. Unsurprisingly, he's also the highest-scoring defender in the club's history and his tally in all competitions is enough to put him in the top 20 of our all-time leading scorers!

Goals: 41
Apps: 492
CFC career: 1998–17
Best PL season:
6 goals (2011/12)

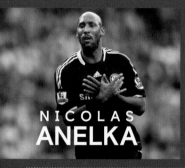

NICOLAS ANELKA

The third player on this list to win the Premier League Golden Boot while at Chelsea, Anelka managed to score 125 goals overall in the competition as he played for six different clubs throughout his career. Thierry Henry is the only Frenchman to score more.

Goals: 38
Apps: 125
CFC career: 2008–12
Best PL season:
19 goals (2008/09)

WILLIAN

Willian just managed to edge out John Spencer, Salomon Kalou and Gus Poyet, who all scored 36 times. The Brazilian was a dead-ball specialist, scoring plenty of his goals from penalties and free-kicks, and he won our Goal of the Season award in 2018 for a beauty against Brighton.

Goals: 37
Apps: 234
CFC career: 2013–20
Best PL season:
9 goals (2019/20)

REECE JAMES

N'GOLO **KANTE**

VIDEO ◄
180

CHELSEA!

The Class
of 1998

<u>DO NOT TAPE OVER!</u> **VHS**

THE CLASS OF

After a 27-year wait for a European trophy, Chelsea picked up two in 1998. A quarter of a century later, we look back on one of the most exciting Blues teams ever to grace Stamford Bridge.

CUP WINNERS CUP WINNERS

From reading that headline you may think we're repeating ourselves, but until 1999 there really was a UEFA competition called the Cup Winners' Cup, and Chelsea won it twice. To enter, you had to win your country's main cup competition, like we did in 1997. Our first success came way back in 1971, when we followed up our FA Cup win the season before by beating Real Madrid in the Cup Winners' Cup final in Athens. Then, in 1998, we repeated the trick. On the way, we beat cup winners from Slovakia, Norway, Spain, Italy and Germany.

OUR LOGO IN 1998

Zola's winning goal in the Cup Winners' Cup final

ZOLA
'THE LITTLE MAGICIAN'

SNOWED UNDER!

Our second opponents, Tromso, played inside the Arctic Circle so it wasn't just freezing cold when we landed in Norway, it even started snowing during the game. By the end of the blizzard, you couldn't see the pitch and we lost 3-2 in the first leg. Luckily for us, the weather was better in London for the second leg, where a 7-1 win took us through to the next round. Gianluca Vialli scored five goals over the two games! The semi-final against Vicenza was one of the most dramatic we've ever played, as we came from two goals down to score three in the second leg. The roar from the fans when Mark Hughes' winner went in made the hairs on the back of your neck stand on end! Our opponents in the final were German side Stuttgart, and thousands of eager Blues fans made the trip to Sweden, where the game took place.

LOADED WITH LEGENDS

Vialli wasn't the only legendary player in that Chelsea team. We also had classy French defender Frank Leboeuf and Italian midfield maestro Roberto Di Matteo, who later won the Champions League as manager of Chelsea in 2012. Then there was captain marvel, Dennis Wise – the cheeky Londoner who held the team together in the middle of the park – and Uruguayan powerhouse Gus Poyet. Vialli's attacking partners that year were the tall and silky Norwegian Tore Andre Flo and one of the greatest players in the history of Chelsea, Gianfranco Zola. Zola was known as 'the little magician' by anyone who saw him play. His close control was faultless and he could score from anywhere inside the opposition half with his fantastic range of shooting. He could take players on, took a mean free-kick and always had a smile for the fans, who loved him as much as anyone ever to wear the Blue shirt.

SUPER CHELSEA

It was Zola who scored the winning goal in the 1998 Cup Winners' Cup final against Stuttgart in Stockholm. The Italian wizard was named as a sub because he was recovering from an injury, but he scored within seconds of coming off the bench with just under 20 minutes to go. He was already a hero, now he was immortal. The win meant that we played Champions League winners Real Madrid in the UEFA Super Cup – our first game against them since that first Cup Winners' Cup final back in 1971. Once again, we ran out 1-0 winners, this time in Monaco's stadium, as Poyet fired home the winning goal with nine minutes left on the clock to win us the trophy for the first time. That year we lived up to the song...
"And it's Super Chelsea, Super Chelsea FC! We're by far the greatest team the world has ever seen!"

Cup Winners' Cup FINAL !!!
Colin + Teresa's wedding
Paul's Christening

THE GOAL
THAT SAVED CHELSEA

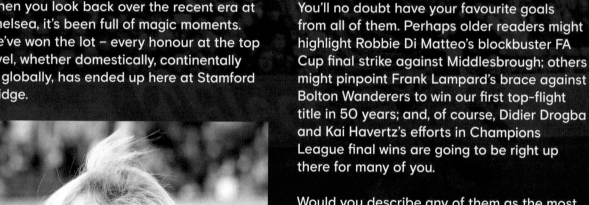

Younger Blues fans have enjoyed a period of unparalleled success
for Chelsea Football Club over the past couple of decades –
but would any of it have been possible without a crucial goal
against Bolton Wanderers 40 seasons ago?

When you look back over the recent era at Chelsea, it's been full of magic moments. We've won the lot – every honour at the top level, whether domestically, continentally or globally, has ended up here at Stamford Bridge.

You'll no doubt have your favourite goals from all of them. Perhaps older readers might highlight Robbie Di Matteo's blockbuster FA Cup final strike against Middlesbrough; others might pinpoint Frank Lampard's brace against Bolton Wanderers to win our first top-flight title in 50 years; and, of course, Didier Drogba and Kai Havertz's efforts in Champions League final wins are going to be right up there for many of you.

Would you describe any of them as the most important goal ever scored by a Chelsea player? Perhaps, but it would be hard to argue for it – after all, without these goals hitting the back of the net, what would the consequences have been? Well, when it comes to a goal Clive Walker scored against Bolton Wanderers on Saturday 7 May 1983, there is a strong case to be made for giving it that title...

Who...is Clive Walker?

Walker was a pacy, exciting winger who in his day could terrorise even the most experienced of defenders – but he was unfortunate to come through the ranks at Chelsea during one of the worst periods in our history. He made a name for himself by scoring spectacular goals, in particular a brilliant effort in an FA Cup win over Liverpool, but the team often found itself languishing in the Second Division and although he still produced moments of magic, including coming off the bench to inspire a comeback from 3-0 down at home to Bolton, it was not a good time to be a Chelsea player. Or, to be fair, a fan...

Why...is his goal so important?

A wet and windy Burnden Park – Bolton's old home ground – played host to what was effectively a relegation play-off between the Blues and the Trotters in the penultimate week of the 1982/83 season. Anything less than a victory would surely put paid to the club's Second Division status with, perhaps, worse to follow than just relegation to the third tier. A match preview in the Daily Mirror newspaper ahead of the game included this ominous sentence: "Rumours suggest the club will be finished if they go down."

What...happened in the game?

A large Blues following – of the 8,687 supporters at Burnden Park that day, the majority were supporting John Neal's side – were present to witness one of the most important moments in our history. A tense game was poised at 0-0 heading towards the final 10 minutes when Walker struck the telling blow with the most important goal of his life. "It was one of those shots that, in that weather, was just about making good contact," he said of the goal years later. "Where the ball hits the net is immaterial

– just make good contact and it'll fly off your boot.

"But it wasn't about who scored the goal, it was all about Chelsea Football Club and stopping them being relegated. I have to say, it was a real team performance and it was helped by a tremendous following – turning up in the pouring rain, the fans were absolutely superb."

Where...did Chelsea go next?

After drawing at Middlesbrough in our final league game of the season we avoided relegation to the third tier of English football, although it was the lowest we have finished in our history – 40th out of 92 clubs in the Football League.

What followed was a remarkable turnaround. Aided by a summer transfer campaign in which we signed several players who went on to become club legends, including Pat Nevin and Kerry Dixon, Neal led us to the Division Two title and back into the top flight.

As for Walker, he started the next season after his Bolton goal in brilliant form, but an injury led to him losing his place in the team and he never regained it. He joined Sunderland a few months later and went on to play more than 1,000 matches in a career that lasted until he was 40. He's now a broadcaster and has long been a presence on Chelsea TV.

WE'VE WON IT ALL!

Chelsea have won the lot when it comes to major silverware, after adding the Club World Cup last year. Let's see how your knowledge stacks up when it comes to the eight biggest trophies we've lifted...

CHAMPIONS LEAGUE

The Blues have been crowned kings of Europe twice, beating Bayern Munich and Manchester City to lift the trophy. Thomas Tuchel was manager for our most recent triumph, but can you remember who was in charge when we won it in 2012?

Answer:

PREMIER LEAGUE

We won our first Premier League title in the 2004/05 season and our most recent in 2016/17. How many times did we get our hands on the trophy in the years between those two triumphs?

Answer:

FA CUP

Chelsea are among the most successful sides in the 150-year history of the FA Cup, winning the trophy eight times. The first was in 1970, when Peter Osgood scored one of the most famous goals in the competition's history as we beat which side?

Answer:

LEAGUE CUP

The second of our five League Cup successes was in 1998, when we beat Middlesbrough in the final. Can you name the Italian who led us to that triumph in only his ninth match as player-manager after taking over from Ruud Gullit?

Answer:

CLUB WORLD CUP

The trophy that completed our clean sweep of honours also happened to crown us as champions of the world. We were pushed all the way in the final by Brazilian side Palmeiras, but who stepped up to convert a penalty in extra time to win the game?

Answer:

EUROPA LEAGUE

Both times we've played in the Europa League we've gone on to win it! The first was in 2013 when we beat Benfica in the final before we repeated the trick in 2019 with a thumping win over Arsenal. Eden Hazard scored twice in his last Chelsea appearance against the Gunners, but what was the final score?

Answer:

UEFA SUPER CUP

A penalty shoot-out was required for the Blues to win our second Super Cup, which came in 2021. Which goalkeeper came on in place of Edouard Mendy in the last minute of extra time and he went on to become the hero?

Answer:

EUROPEAN CUP WINNERS' CUP

You might not remember this trophy, as the last edition took place in 1999 before it merged with the UEFA Cup, which later became the Europa League. We won it for the second time in 1998 when Gianfranco Zola came off the bench to score the winner against VfB Stuttgart, but can you tell us how many seconds he had been on the pitch when the ball hit the back of the net?

Answer:

○ a) 5   ○ b) 21   ○ c) 60

Answers on p63

Chelsea FC Stadium Tours & Museum

Experience the unforgettable, behind-the-scenes Stamford Bridge Stadium Tour & Museum.

Search CFC Tours

THE PRIDE OF LONDON

10 TOP CHELSEA FACTS

Who scored the most goals, who played most games, who won the most titles? It's time to find out all about Chelsea's record breakers and history makers through the ages...

RECORD VICTORY

Our biggest-ever win came in a European Cup Winners' Cup tie against Jeunesse Hautcharage, from Luxembourg, in September 1971. Chelsea won the home leg 13-0 and we've never won by more goals. Our biggest league win was 8-0 at home to Wigan Athletic in May 2010, on the day we won the Premier League title!

RECORD DEFEAT

Our worst-ever loss came in a league match away at Wolves in September 1953, when we were beaten 8-1 by our hosts, who went on to win the league that season. We can't have been that bad because we finished eighth and then became champions the following season! Chelsea have also lost 7-0 twice, to Leeds United in October 1967 and to Nottingham Forest in April 1991.

MOST CLEAN SHEETS

Nobody has kept more clean sheets for Chelsea than Petr Cech, who managed not to concede a goal in 228 of his 494 games for the club between 2004 and 2015.

TOP GOALSCORER

Frank Lampard is Chelsea's all-time top goalscorer, with 211 goals. He scored them in a 13-year spell with the club between 2001 and 2014, in which time he played 648 games.

MOST GOALS IN A SEASON

Jimmy Greaves scored the most goals for Chelsea in a single season when he hit the back of the net 43 times in all competitions in the 1960/61 campaign. He played 43 games that season, meaning he averaged a goal every game!

MOST APPEARANCES

Ron Harris played 795 games for Chelsea between 1961 and 1980, which remains a record to this day. He was captain for 324 of those games.

MOST GAMES AS CAPTAIN

The record for most games as captain belongs to John Terry, who skippered the side 580 times in his 717 appearances for Chelsea.

MOST HONOURS

Terry has also won the most trophies with Chelsea, having picked up 17 major honours as a Blues player. JT has won the most league titles with the club too, as he has five Premier League winners' medals to his name.

JIMMY GREAVES!

RECORD ATTENDANCE

Our biggest-ever crowd for an official home game was 82,905 for a league tie against Arsenal, on 12 October 1935. However, it is believed that more than 100,000 were inside Stamford Bridge for a friendly game against Dynamo Moscow in November 1945, but no official record of the attendance for that match exists.

100,000+ SUPPORTERS

LONGEST-SERVING MANAGER

David Calderhead was Chelsea manager for an incredible 25 years and 280 days between 1 August 1907 and 8 May 1933, making him by far and away our longest-serving manager ever.

IT'S A
CHELSEA
THING

2022/23

HOME KIT

**VISIT THE OFFICIAL
ONLINE MEGASTORE TO
GET YOUR 2022/23 KITS
AND A FULL RANGE OF
CHELSEA FC PRODUCTS.**

WWW.CHELSEAMEGASTORE.COM

SP QT THE DIFFERENCE

Can you spot the **EIGHT** differences between these two pictures of the team celebrating Jorginho's goal against Everton at the start of the season?

Answers on p63

BETHANY ENGLAND

NATIONAL PRIDE

QUIZ!

1 The Blues' legendary goalkeeper Peter Bonetti was part of England's only World Cup-winning squad. But do you know the year when The Cat and his team-mates got their hands on the Jules Rimet trophy?

2 Prior to Qatar 2022, the last men's World Cup was held in Russia, when two Chelsea players were victorious as part of the French squad. N'Golo Kante was one of them, but can you name the other?

3 Chelsea duo Jorginho and Emerson helped Italy to the men's Euro in 2021, which was played across Europe, but can you remember which stadium hosted the final against England?

4 Can you tell us which member of our trio of European Championship winners with France in 2000 made the fewest appearances for Chelsea: Marcel Desailly, Didier Deschamps or Frank Leboeuf?

5 Crystal Dunn was in the last squad to win the Women's World Cup. Can you tell us which country she represented?

6 Which Chelsea striker won the Golden Boot at the men's Euro in 2012 after helping Spain retain the trophy?

7 Do you know the current Chelsea Women midfielder who won both a European Championship and an Olympic gold medal with the German national team?

8 Andre Schurrle was a men's World Cup winner for Germany in 2014 and he scored twice in a famous 7-1 win over which country in the semi-finals?

Answers on p63

CELEBRATE GOOD TIMES!

The euphoric moment when the ball hits the back of the net is often followed by an iconic celebration, as emotion takes over and it all comes pouring out. Sometimes they are spectacular, occasionally humorous, but it's always a moment that we, as fans and players, share together...

SKY'S THE LIMIT

When Roberto Di Matteo scored his first Chelsea goal, he dropped to the turf and pointed to the sky. Soon he was joined by a group of team-mates in this apparently unchoreographed celebration, although if there had been any rehearsals they were clearly missed by Frank Leboeuf (pictured on the left)!

JUST DANCE

After chipping Victor Valdes to score an extraordinary goal at the Nou Camp in front of 90,000 fans, the normally reserved Ramires decided to pull out some of his best dance moves!

ACROBATICS

Celestine Babayaro endeared himself to Chelsea fans in the late Nineties by celebrating his goals with a backflip, a tradition that lives on among Blues today thanks to Sam Kerr, who occasionally pulls out her trademark acrobatics to the delight of the Kingsmeadow crowd.

BOLT FROM THE BLUE

Fernando Torres marked his opener in the 2013 Europa League final by 'Bolting', the term given to Usain Bolt's trademark celebration. Zero marks for originality, but probably a better choice than the Mo-bot...

HOMAGE TO DAD

Frank Lampard scored a wonder goal to win us the 2009 FA Cup final – and he marked the occasion by celebrating just like his dad did 29 years earlier after scoring against the Toffees in an FA Cup semi-final, by dancing around the corner flag.

BAND PRACTICE

Didier Drogba and Florent Malouda formed an impromptu 'Blues' band after Drog was on target in a thumping 8-0 win over Wigan Athletic to clinch the Premier League title on the final day of the 2009/10 season.

BACK BANTER

After Jose Mourinho had commented on his age, Samuel Eto'o got his own back – get it? – on the manager by celebrating his next goal with a pretend walking stick!

SHINING STAR

This is a classic of the Premier League era, shown off here by Branislav Ivanovic but we could have chosen from any number of players who have pulled this out. Stick your boot up in the air and wait for one of your team-mates to come over and give it a shine!

KEEP YOUR SHORTS ON!

One celebration we cannot recommend is this one from Frank Sinclair, who scored against Coventry City on the opening day of the 1997/98 season and promptly dropped his shorts. His team-mates found it hilarious, but the FA weren't so keen as they fined him!

FAN-TASTIC

Sometimes, though, the best celebrations are the ones where it's just about pure emotion. John Terry's last-gasp equaliser against Everton in 2016 was one such moment when it all came roaring out...

MAGDALENA **ERIKSSON**